SCENE BY SCENE COMPARATIVE WORKBOOKS

The King's Speech

by Tom Hooper

Social Setting

Relationships

Hero, Heroine, Villain

Copyright © 2015 by Amy Farrell.

All rights reserved. No part of this publication may be reproduced, distributed or transmitted in any form or by any means, including photocopying, recording, or other electronic or mechanical methods, without the prior written permission of the publisher, except in the case of brief quotations embodied in critical reviews and certain other noncommercial uses permitted by copyright law. For permission requests, write to the publisher, addressed "Attention: Permissions Coordinator," at the address below.

Scene by Scene
11 Millfield, Enniskerry
Wicklow, Ireland.
www.scenebysceneguides.com

orders@scenebyscene.ie

The King's Speech Comparative Workbook OL16 by Amy Farrell. —1st ed.
ISBN 978-1-910949-09-2

2016 Ordinary Level Comparative Workbook

'The King's Speech' by Tom Hooper

The modes at Ordinary Level for 2016 are:

Social Setting

This mode refers to the setting and social world of the text.

Consider the roles of men and women, race, religion, social class, etc.

Relationships

This mode refers to the relationships between characters in the story.

Consider whether relationships are difficult, if they make characters happy or unhappy, their importance in the story, etc.

Hero, Heroine, Villain

This mode refers to the study and analysis of a specific lead character.

Consider the character's personality, behavior, what you like and dislike about them, etc.

The King's Speech by Tom Hooper
Social Setting

THE KING'S SPEECH - SOCIAL SETTING

Where does the story take place? Describe the locations where the action takes place. Use quotes/examples to support your points.

When does the story take place? Use quotes/examples to support your points.

KNOW THE TEXT

What is life like for the Royal Family? Mention their **privileges** and **responsibilities**.

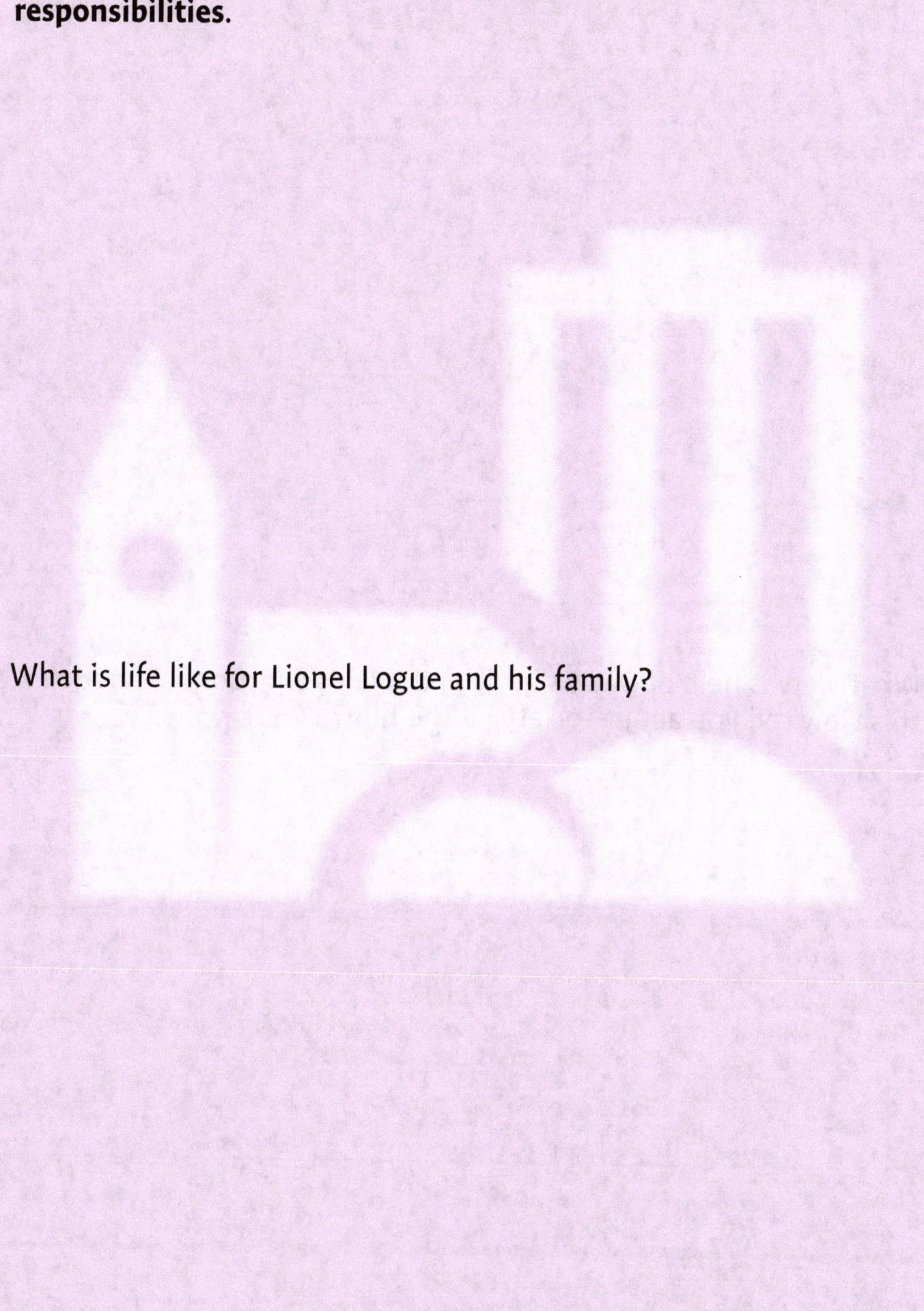

What is life like for Lionel Logue and his family?

THE KING'S SPEECH - SOCIAL SETTING

Why is Bertie's stammer such a problem for him?

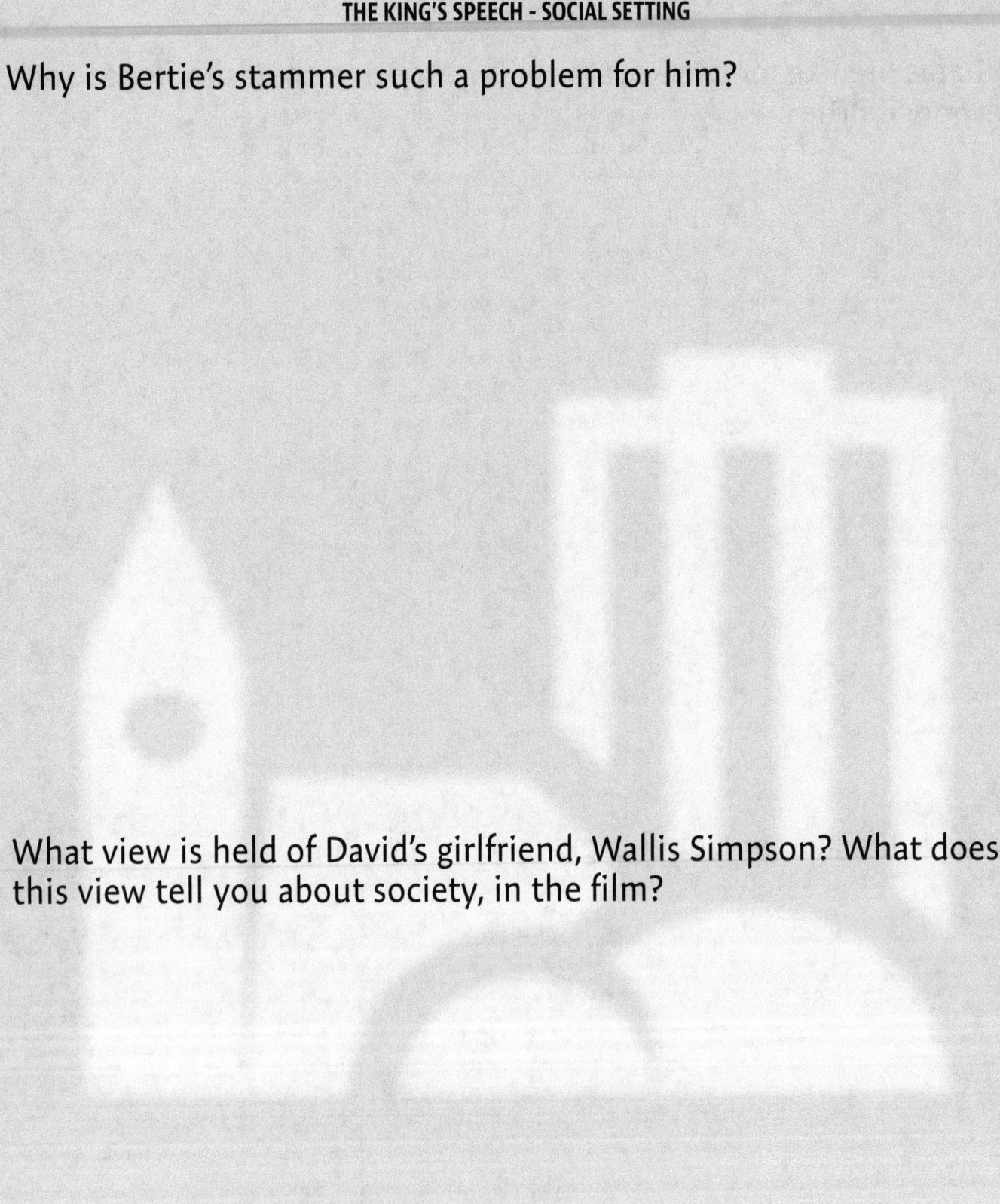

What view is held of David's girlfriend, Wallis Simpson? What does this view tell you about society, in the film?

KNOW THE TEXT

Why does David, Bertie's brother, abdicate? What does this tell you about society, in the film?

Explain the threat of **war** in the film.

THE KING'S SPEECH - SOCIAL SETTING

Is the world of this film a **formal** place? Explain.

What role does Elizabeth, Bertie's wife, have?

KNOW THE TEXT

How does Bertie treat his wife? Use quotes/examples to support your view.

What is the role of **women** in this film?

THE KING'S SPEECH - SOCIAL SETTING

What **religious** role does the King of England have?

Are members of the Royal Family warm and loving or stiff and formal towards one another? What does this tell you about the Social Setting?

KNOW THE TEXT

Do Bertie and Lionel have a good friendship?

Are **class differences** important to Bertie?

What does Bertie value in life?

What does Lionel value in life?

THE KING'S SPEECH - SOCIAL SETTING

Describe the **setting** of this text.

KNOW THE MODE

What is the **role of women** in this text?

THE KING'S SPEECH - SOCIAL SETTING

What is the **role of men** in this story?

KNOW THE MODE

How are **children treated** in the world of this story?

THE KING'S SPEECH - SOCIAL SETTING

Is **family** important to the characters in this story?

KNOW THE MODE

Is **religion** important to the characters in this story?

Do the characters in this story hold **traditional beliefs**?

KNOW THE MODE

Is the setting of this text a **violent** or **peaceful** place?

THE KING'S SPEECH - SOCIAL SETTING

Is this a **secure** or **dangerous** world?

KNOW THE MODE

Where do you see **conflict** in this text?

THE KING'S SPEECH - SOCIAL SETTING

How are **characters affected** by the Social Setting of this story?

KNOW THE MODE

Would you like to live in the world of this text? Why/why not?

THE KING'S SPEECH - SOCIAL SETTING

Choose key moments from the film that **highlight the Social Setting** of the text.

KNOW THE MODE

THE KING'S SPEECH - SOCIAL SETTING

What **similarities** do you notice between the Social Setting of this text and your other comparative texts?

KNOW THE MODE

THE KING'S SPEECH - SOCIAL SETTING

What **differences** do you notice between the Social Setting of this text and your other comparative texts?

KNOW THE MODE

33

THE KING'S SPEECH - SOCIAL SETTING

The King's Speech by Tom Hooper
Relationships

THE KING'S SPEECH - RELATIONSHIPS

Does Elizabeth care about her husband, Bertie?

Does she understand him?

Does Bertie care about his wife?

KNOW THE TEXT

Does he understand her?

What strengths do you see in Bertie's marriage to Elizabeth?

What weaknesses do you see in Bertie's marriage to Elizabeth?

Describe Bertie's relationship with his father.

What causes problems in this relationship?

Describe Bertie's relationship with his brother, David.

KNOW THE TEXT

What causes problems in this relationship?

Are Bertie's relationships with his family positive or negative?

How does Bertie treat his children?

THE KING'S SPEECH - RELATIONSHIPS

How does Bertie treat Lionel at first?

How does Lionel treat Bertie at first?

What barriers are there to their friendship?

KNOW THE TEXT

How does their relationship change and develop?

What causes them to argue?

How do they resolve their differences?

THE KING'S SPEECH - RELATIONSHIPS

Is this friendship important to these men?

Do they have a good relationship?

What strengths do you see in Bertie's friendship with Lionel?

KNOW THE TEXT

What weaknesses do you see in Bertie's friendship with Lionel?

What impact does this friendship have on Bertie?

Does this friendship bring Bertie and Lionel happiness?

THE KING'S SPEECH - RELATIONSHIPS

KNOW THE MODE

Are relationships **generally positive** (warm, supportive, nurturing, genuine) or **negative** (cold, cruel, destructive, false) in the film?

THE KING'S SPEECH - RELATIONSHIPS

What makes relationships in the story **difficult**?

KNOW THE MODE

What would improve relationships in the film?

THE KING'S SPEECH - RELATIONSHIPS

How do relationships **change** during the film?

KNOW THE MODE

Does this film teach us anything about relationships?

KNOW THE MODE

Does this film teach us anything about relationships?

What is the **most important** relationship in the film? What makes it so important?

KNOW THE MODE

Do relationships in the film bring characters **happiness** or **unhappiness**?

THE KING'S SPEECH - RELATIONSHIPS

Choose **key moments** from the film that **highlight Relationships** in the text.

KNOW THE MODE

THE KING'S SPEECH - RELATIONSHIPS

What **similarities** do you notice in the Relationships of this text and your other comparative texts?

KNOW THE MODE

THE KING'S SPEECH - RELATIONSHIPS

What **differences** do you notice in the Relationships of this text and your other comparative texts?

KNOW THE MODE

KNOW THE MODE

The King's Speech by Tom Hooper
Hero, Heroine, Villain

KNOW THE TEXT

Describe Bertie, the **hero** of this film.

What are his **strengths**? (his good/strong points)

THE KING'S SPEECH - HERO, HEROINE, VILLAIN

What are his **weaknesses**? (his flaws/weak points)

What **problems** does he face?

KNOW THE TEXT

Does he overcome these problems? Why/why not?

Why is Bertie reluctant to be King?

THE KING'S SPEECH - HERO, HEROINE, VILLAIN

Is Bertie **brave** (heroic) in this story? Explain your view.

Do you feel sympathy for Bertie? Explain your view.

KNOW THE TEXT

Is Bertie a good friend, in this film?

How did Bertie change, during the course of the story?

THE KING'S SPEECH - HERO, HEROINE, VILLAIN

As the film ends, do you think he will make a good King?

KNOW THE TEXT

What did you **like** about Bertie, the central character in this film?

KNOW THE MODE

What did you **dislike** about this character?

Is he an **emotional** character? Use examples to support your view.

KNOW THE MODE

What do you **admire** about Bertie?

THE KING'S SPEECH - HERO, HEROINE, VILLAIN

Is this character a **hero or villain**? Explain your choice.

KNOW THE MODE

On a scale of one to ten, with one being an extremely heroic character and ten being an evil villain, where would you place Bertie? Explain your choice.

Overall, did you **like** this character? Explain your opinion.

KNOW THE MODE

Is Bertie happy or sad?

Would you like to meet him?

KNOW THE MODE

If you met him, what would you talk about?

What advice would you give him, if you met him?

KNOW THE MODE

Is he a 'good' (successful/interesting) main character?

Identify the **key moments** in the film that illustrate Bertie's personality/character.

KNOW THE MODE

THE KING'S SPEECH - HERO, HEROINE, VILLAIN

How is Bertie **similar** to the Hero, Heroine, Villain in your other texts?

KNOW THE MODE

KNOW THE MODE

THE KING'S SPEECH - HERO, HEROINE, VILLAIN

How is Bertie **different** to the Hero, Heroine, Villain in your other texts?

KNOW THE MODE